photo**word**book

My body

Sue Barraclough

WAYLAND

First published in 2007 by Wayland

Copyright © Wayland 2007

Wayland
338 Euston Road
London NW1 3BH

Wayland Australia
Level 17/207 Kent Street
Sydney, NSW 2000

Design: Natascha Frensch
Typography: Natascha Frensch
Read Regular (European Community Design Registration 2003)
Read Regular and Read Xheavy copyright © Natascha Frensch 2001-2006

Editor: Joyce Bentley
Picture research: Sue Barraclough
Photography: Paul Bricknell

ISBN 978 0 7502 5151 8

Printed in China

Wayland is a division of Hachette Children's Books, an Hachette Livre UK company.

Acknowledgements: Cover © Laureen Morgane/Corbis; p 1 Mike Powell/Taxi/Getty

2

Contents

3

body

I have a **body**.

arm

foot

4

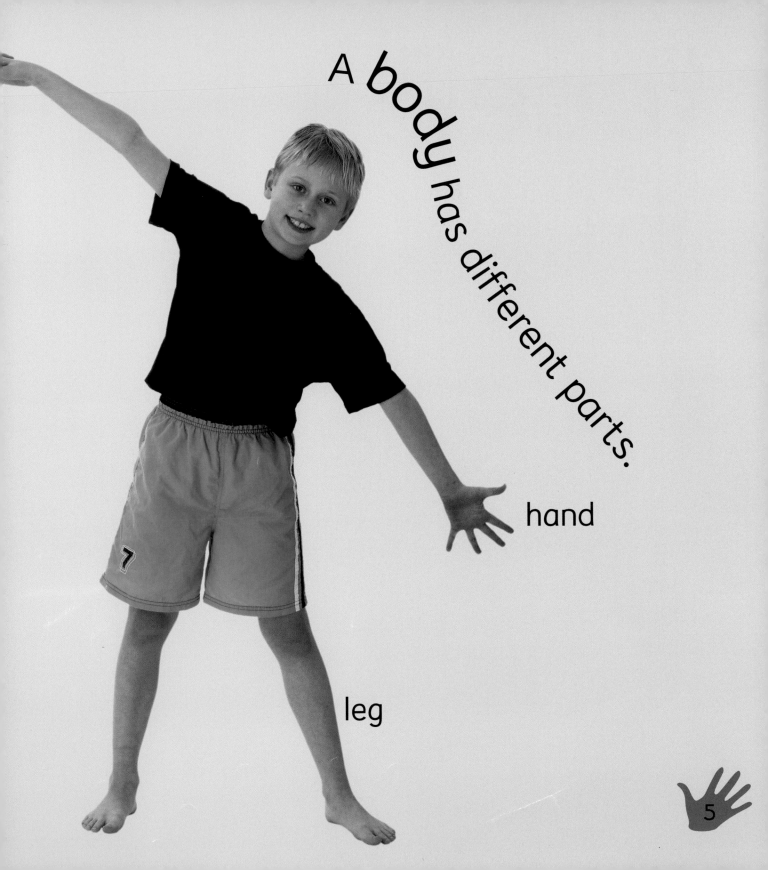

A **body** has different parts.

hand

leg

5

face

I have a **face**.

I can make funny **faces**.

eyes

I have two **eyes**.

I use my **eyes** to see.

nose

I have a **nose**.

We smell things with our **noses**.

9

mouth

I have a **mouth**.

I use my **mouth** to speak.

ears

I have two **ears**.

I hear with my ears.

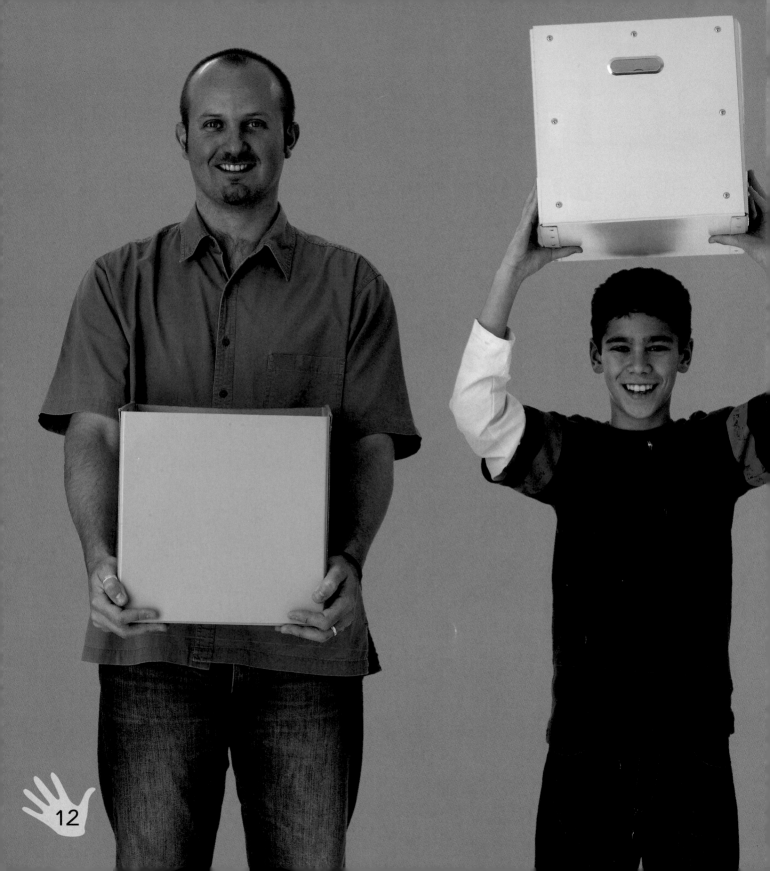

arms

I have two **arms**.

We carry things with our **arms**.

hands

I have two hands.

I can hold things in my hand.

15

legs

I have two **legs**.

We use our legs for walking.

17

feet

I have two **feet**.

I can stand on one **foot**.

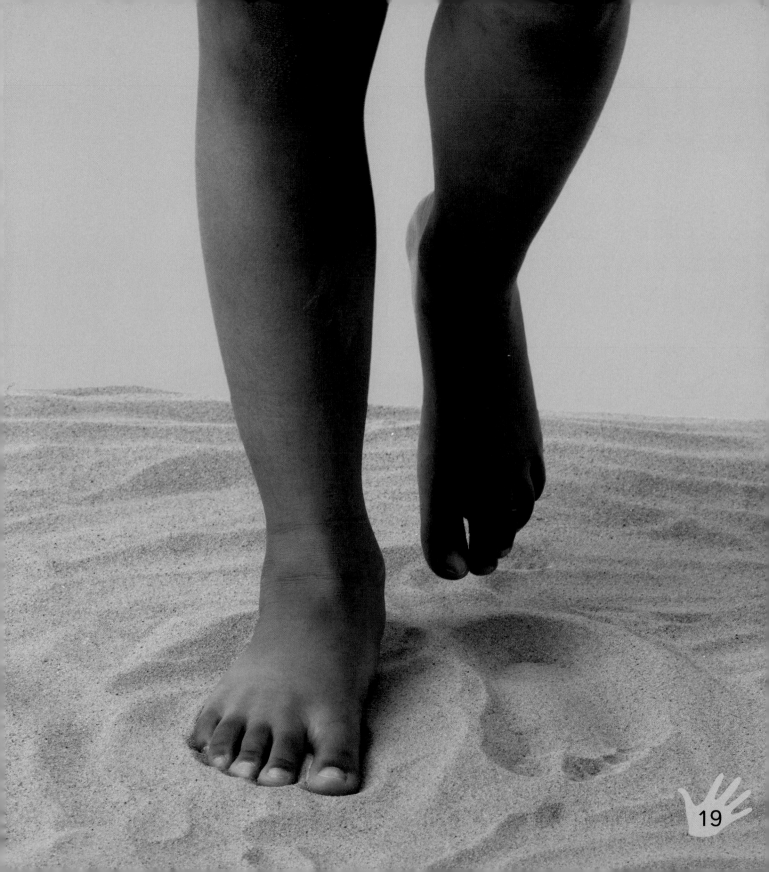

toes

I have **toes.**

We have ten ticklish **toes** each!

Picture quiz

Can you find these words in the book?

smell

hear

speak

see

What pages are they on?

22

Index quiz

The index is on page 24.
Use the index and pictures
to answer these questions.

1. Which page shows a funny face?
   What colour is the boy's hair?

2. Which pages show six legs?
   How many boots can you count?

3. Which page shows smelly flowers?
   What colour are the flowers?

4. Which pages show ticklish toes?
   How many big toes can you count?

23

Index

arms 4, 13

body 4, 5

ears 11

eyes 8

face 6

feet 4, 18

hands 5, 14

hear 11

legs 5, 16, 17

mouth 10

nose 9

see 8

smell 9

speak 10

toes 20, 21

Answers
Picture quiz: Smell is on page 9, Hear is on page 11, Speak is on page 10, See is on page 8.
Index quiz: 1. page 7, black; 2. pages 16-17, four; 3. page 9, yellow; 4. pages 20-21, six.